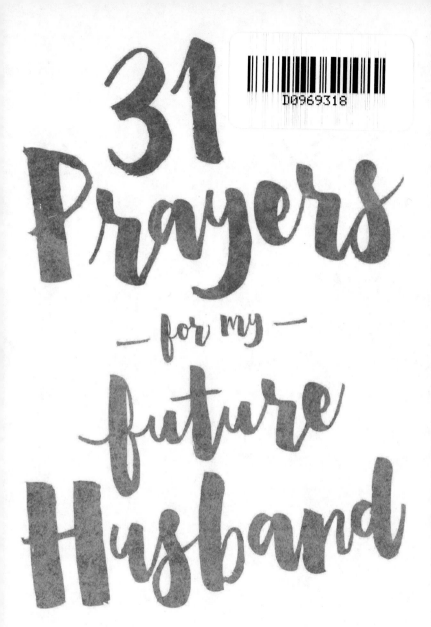

31 Prayers

— for my —

future

Husband

PREPARING MY HEART FOR MARRIAGE
BY PRAYING FOR HIM

JENNIFER & AARON SMITH

31 Prayers For My Future Husband

Preparing My Heart For Marriage By Praying For Him

Written By Jennifer & Aaron Smith
Edited By Cambria Jacobson & Stacy Mehan
Cover & Interior Design By Jane Johnson
Interior Format & Layout By Aaron Smith

ISBN: 0-9863667-5-7
ISBN 13: 978-0-9863667-5-8
LCCN: 2016915321

31prayersformyfuturehusband.com

Printed in U.S.A

31 Prayers For My Future Husband

Contents

God Hears Us — 7

Introduction — 9

His Heart — 16

Challenge #1 — **20**

His Family — 22

His Words — 26

Protecting His Mind — 30

Challenge #2 — **34**

Understanding His Purpose — 36

Confidence In You — 40

Staying Out Of Debt — 46

Making Wise Decisions — 50

Challenge #3 — **54**

His Health — 56

Integrity — 60

Resisting Temptation — 64

Love Like Christ — 70

Being A Good Steward — 74

Challenge #4 — **78**

Good Company — 80

Saying No To Pornography — 84

Dying To Self — 88

Working Hard — 94

Striving For Purity — 98

A Heart Of Compassion — 102

Challenge #5 — **106**

Victory In Christ — 108

Becoming A Leader — 112

Relinquishing Worries — 116

Living w/ Understanding — 122

Fruit Of The Spirit — 126

Maturing Him — 130

Challenge #6 — **134**

Humility — 136

Preparing His Heart — 140

Intimacy With God — 144

Our Future Wedding — 150

Our Future Marriage — 154

Our Future Oneness — 158

Challenge #7 — **162**

Vows — 166

Resources — 173

God Hears Us

1 John 5:13-15

"I write these things to you who believe in the name of the Son of God, that you may know that you have eternal life. And this is the confidence that we have toward him, that if we ask anything according to his will he hears us. And if we know that he hears us in whatever we ask, we know that we have the requests that we have asked of him."

31 Prayers For My Future Husband

Introduction

Marriage is a beautiful relationship that unifies two individuals, binding them together through their commitment to love each other, making them one. There is no other relationship on earth that can compare to the intimacy experienced in marriage as God designed it. Just like we become one with Jesus when we accept Him into our hearts, married together through a powerful covenant which He sacrificed Himself to provide, marriage is a reflection of this miraculous oneness. A husband and wife reflect that same love that motivated Christ when they love each other. They die to themselves and become one.

I longed to become a wife. As much as I desired to be the perfect wife and a helper for my future husband, I had a few selfish intentions that motivated my desire to get married. I was terrified of living life alone, I was desperate to feel loved by a man because of a lack of security in my relationship with my father and I craved the experience of sex because I was abstaining in pursuit of purity. I thought a husband would satisfy me completely. With these things reigning in my heart and fear pushing me forward, I made decisions that were selfish and ones that did not align with God's will for my life.

On the other hand, I was praying faithfully for my future husband. No matter what situations I got myself into, I believed God would provide for me a good husband. It was my commitment to prayer that transformed my perspective of marriage, the choices I was making and my selfish motives.

I felt like God told me, "I can't trust you with someone else's heart until you trust me with yours."

So I focused on my relationship with God and began to trust Him. I also kept praying for my future husband. I looked forward to the day I would marry my best friend, even though I didn't know who that was at the time. I prayed for his heart, for his mind, for protection and for our future together.

When my best friend, Aaron, proposed marriage to me, he did it by showing me his hand-written prayers dated back before we even met, prayers for his future wife! Then he told me that I was his answer to those prayers.

Becoming a bride and knowing that God brought my husband and I together has been one of the best feelings in the world. There have been moments where I wrestled with insecurities that have been with me since childhood, but the Lord has been faithful to answer both of our prayers for each other and for our marriage. Prayer has also been the most powerful tool in saving and strengthening our marriage!

My husband and I can personally testify to the power of prayer, which is why we encourage others to have a heart dedicated to prayer. Through our online ministries (Unveiled Wife & Husband Revolution) we kept hearing one couple after another admit how difficult prayer is, how uncomfortable it is to pray for each other and we have heard that some people just don't know how to pray. Hearing these stories moved us to write Thirty-One Prayers For My Wife and Thirty-One Prayers For My Husband. The feedback we receive from couples taking our 31 Prayer Challenge has been astounding. Testimonies continue to flood in from husbands and wives about how God is moving in their hearts and marriages.

We praise God for the breakthroughs marriages are experiencing because of these resources. However, there was this thought in the back of our minds about encouraging people to become prayer warriors before the wedding! We thought about the next generation of husbands and wives that need to know how to pray for each other and their relationship. We hope 31 Prayers For My Future Husband and 31 Prayers For My Future

Wife inspire people's hearts to commit to praying for the marriage they hope to one day have or the marriage they are in the process of planning for right now. Our heart's desire is to see men and women prepare their hearts for marriage by praying and petitioning to God for the hearts of their future spouse. We hope and pray people who desire to have a God-centered marriage will take this prayer challenge to equip them for their future marriage.

We wrote this book because we want to help you and motivate you to pray for the husband you long for. We want you to be open and willing to pray for your future marriage. Most of all we want you to draw closer to God through the power of prayer! We also desire that when you do become a wife, you will have such a strong, passionate and established prayer life, that the enemy can't knock you down.

This resource is not a magical book that will produce your future husband. Reading this book and praying these prayers will not guarantee that you will one day get married. However, the Bible is clear that we are to come to God and pray for everything.

"Do not be anxious about anything, but in everything by prayer and supplication with thanksgiving let your requests be made known to God." - Philippians 4:6 ESV

Praying for a future marriage that you hope for, will remind your heart not to worry, but rather trust in God and in His timing. Praying for your future husband is a request that God asks you to make known to Him. By faithfully praying for your future husband and future marriage, you are unveiling your heart to God and letting Him get to know you! Growing close to God, trusting Him with your heart, knowing Him and being known by Him is true intimacy!

As you submit your heart to God in prayer, you will see Him move! And oh how wonderful it will be to one day hear a testimony from your future husband about how your prayers helped him! You can read these prayers straight from the text, you can say them out loud, you can get on your knees or stand with your hands raised up toward the sky. There are also journal lines provided to make these prayers personal to you. You are God's daughter and He is going to be blessed hearing from you!

I have included a few challenges to encourage you to consider the significance and purpose of prayer. There is a total of 7 challenges and I urge you to pray about each one and then fulfill it as the Lord leads you.

****I would love to see your journey along the way! Update your social media and tag @unveiledwife and #UW31Prayers so I can follow along and see how God is moving in your life!****

Dear Heavenly Father,

Thank You for the woman reading this book. Anoint her as she experiences the power of prayer. Speak gently to her and affirm her heart. Reveal Yourself to her in mighty ways. May Your Holy Spirit lead her through each prayer and inspire her to pray for even more than what she finds in this book. May she mature into a prayer warrior, petitioning for her future marriage. Lord, if it is in Your will that she gets married, give her patience until that sweet day comes. Fulfill her and satisfy her heart completely. Help her to trust in You for all things. Bless this woman for her faithfulness!

In Jesus' name AMEN!

His Heart

Mark 12:30

Dear Lord,

I pray for my future husband. I pray for his heart. May You continue to mature him and reveal Yourself to him in mighty ways. I pray that he would love You passionately. May You and him have an incredibly deep relationship. I pray he is willing to open his heart to You. I pray he comes to You in prayer and is vulnerable about the things he is facing in this life. I pray he relies on You for help and guidance. Fill him with Your wisdom. I pray a blessing over his heart. I also pray for protection. Please remove any temptation or evil that is attempting to make him fall or get hurt or turn from You. Guard his heart and cover him with Your peace. If there are any situations or circumstances that cause him pain, I pray that You would heal him. Make his heart whole. I pray my future husband would have a strong understanding of who You are and how You are moving in his life. I pray his heart is full of discernment and is sensitive to Your Holy Spirit. I pray that he is willing to address his emotions and doesn't push them away. Soften his heart so that he is always willing to yield to You in humbleness. I also pray that he would embrace all that You have for him and that he is passionate to serve You joyfully. May You continue to experience intimacy with him. I pray he loves You with all of his heart, all of his soul, all of his mind and all of his strength.

In Jesus' name AMEN!

Personalize

Use this area to write a personalized prayer for your future husband. You can also write a list of things you would like to continue to pray for.

Challenge

— #1 —

START A
prayer journal

Use this journal to write down your prayers,
especially your prayers for your future husband.

Begin your prayer journal by writing out
a personal prayer for your future husband.

His Family

Exodus 20:12

Dear God,

I pray my future husband honors his mother and father. I pray that they have a strong and healthy relationship. If they have any painful wounds in their relationship, please heal them and help them reconcile. If they need to forgive each other, I pray that they can forgive and extend grace to each other. I pray that my future husband would talk to his parents and other family members with respect. I pray he is kind, caring and compassionate with them. I also pray that he is bold with them and capable of talking about difficult matters with courage and strength. I pray he honors his family, but when the time comes to be my husband, he would be able to balance the priority of our marriage over his family in a respectful way. I pray my future husband is able to have healthy boundaries with his family. I pray they are a loving family and that they love You. I pray he learns how to be a good husband because of the example of his father. If his father is absent or not a good example, I pray You would bring someone into his life who would teach him how to fulfill his role as a husband and as a father. May You bless my future husband's relationships with his family and may he be a light of the gospel to them always.

In Jesus' name AMEN!

Personalize

Use this area to write a personalized prayer for your future husband. You can also write a list of things you would like to continue to pray for.

His Words

Luke 6:45

Dear Heavenly Father,

Thank You for my future husband. I pray that he is a reputable man. I pray he is looked up to by his peers in high regard. I pray that his character is a reflection of You. May You anoint his speech and every word that comes out of his mouth. I pray my future husband has a conviction to have control over his tongue and is quick to use his words to affirm others. I pray he never uses his words to bring people down or hurt them. I pray that the treasure in his heart produces good fruit that is evident to all. I also pray his words are a true reflection of what is in his heart. Convict his heart of lying or manipulating. I pray he speaks the truth in every situation. I pray he can clearly communicate with others with utmost respect. I pray he has a desire to communicate with others, so that in our marriage he is able to clearly, calmly and respectfully communicate with me. I pray he uses his words to encourage me and comfort me in times of need. I pray his words would always land softly upon my heart. I pray he is open with me and is able to share with me what is on his heart. I pray we would experience a beautiful and harmonious relationship because of our ability to communicate with each other. I pray that he is willing to use his words to pray out loud with me and that he is willing to praise You out loud. I pray he leads our relationship with a gentleness in his tone of voice and love motivating his every word.

In Jesus' name AMEN!

Protecting His Mind

Romans 12:2

Dear Lord,

I pray You would protect my future husband's mind. I pray he would be strong to fight against temptations. I pray he would rely on You for strength, for wisdom, for everything. I pray You would reveal Yourself to him in mighty ways so that his faith continues to grow. May Your Word be a foundation in his heart. I pray You would renew him by Your Word. I pray he would be transformed into the man You created him to be. If there are parts of his character that need to be transformed, I pray he would surrender to You and allow You to change him. In this world full of hatred, evil and sin, may he walk in a pattern of righteousness. Build him up so that he walks in spiritual maturity. Do not let any pressure burden him or tempt him to sin. May Your Holy Spirit guide him, comfort him and teach him. Fill him with confidence so that insecurities and doubt do not overtake him. I pray he would not wrestle with depression or discontentment. May he know that You love him and care about every detail of his life. I pray his mind is focused and purposed on doing Your will. Remove any distractions from his life that are creating chaos for him. May You guard my future husband in all ways. Protect him from the evil in this world. Keep him safe. May he find his security in You and You alone.

In Jesus' name AMEN!

Challenge

— #2 —

TAKE SOME
time to think

Consider all the ways God shows you His love.

Praise Him for all the intentional details
He puts into the thoughtful and caring
ways He loves you.

Understanding His Purpose

Psalm 57:2

Dear Lord,

Thank You for today. Thank You for the gift of life. I lift up my future husband to You. Thank You for his life. Thank You for his purpose. May You reveal to him what his purpose is and why You created him. Show him that his life's worth living. I pray my future husband is talented, I pray he is always gaining new skills and I pray he is passionate about the work that he does. Holy Spirit, please show him how to fulfill his purpose. Reveal to him what his gifts are. Show him how You can use him to bless others and build up Your Kingdom. Satisfy his heart and help him to be content. Inspire him to always look to the future. Give him hope in the plans You have for him. I also pray he would be hopeful for our relationship, understanding the significant purpose marriage has. I pray against feelings of unworthiness. I pray against feelings of inadequacies. I pray against fear and insecurity. I pray my future husband never wrestles with depression and I pray he is never consumed by negative thoughts that try to convince him that his life does not matter. Provide encouragements and affirmations daily, to remind him that You created him with extraordinary purpose. Send him encouragement and affirmation today. Remind him that You created him with extraordinary purpose. I pray my future husband knows confidently what his purpose is and that You have fully equipped him to carry out that purpose.

In Jesus' name AMEN!

Confidence In You

Jeremiah 17:7

Dear Lord,

Thank You for this day. Wherever my future husband is and no matter what he is doing, I pray that he feels You near. May Your presence bring a peace that washes over him. I pray he has an incredible day. Fill his heart with joy that is indescribable. I pray he has confidence in You. I pray he trusts in You for everything and in every circumstance he faces. I pray he leans on Your wisdom to guide him and that he trusts Your will for his life. Bless him for trusting in You. Build up his confidence in You. I pray he learns how to trust You now, so as a husband when he leads me he would do so without doubt or fear clouding his mind. I pray my future husband does not crumble under the pressures of this world. I pray he doesn't strive after achieving what the world's standard of good is, but rather, I pray he would pursue You and strive to live out all that You have called him to. When the world's advice is different or contrary to Your Word, I pray he would trust You enough to follow Your truth. I pray against the persuasion of the enemy. I pray against lies and deceit. Help my future husband to know the difference between the enemy's lies and Your truth. May his fear of You be greater than anything else in this world. May he stand firm on truth, may he walk in integrity and may he live with mighty confidence in You.

In Jesus' name AMEN!

Unveil
Hear

Your

t

Unveiling your heart to God means that you are willing to share everything with Him. What are you feeling, why are you feeling that way, what are your needs and desires? Being transparent with God will cultivate intimacy with Him and it help you to be open and transparent with your future husband.

Staying Out Of Debt

Romans 13:8

Dear Lord,

Thank You for Your provision. Your love is never-ending! I pray for my future husband. May Your Holy Spirit guide him with financial decisions. I pray he would be a good steward of every resource and provision You have blessed him with. I pray he is strongly convicted to stay out of debt. I pray every choice he makes is founded on Your wisdom, Your truth and what Your Word says about finances. May Your Holy Spirit teach him how to navigate decisions requiring financial astuteness. May his heart be sensitive to Your Holy Spirit, yielding in a submissive way to how You desire him to spend money. I pray he reacts with caution toward any purchase he makes. I pray his convictions even inspire his friends and family to live debt free. May others see Your blessing in his life and how staying out of debt is incredibly beneficial. May they commit to living debt free and may they also reap the benefits of being good stewards with all that You give them. This world is backwards when it comes to finances and the enemy has persuaded people to be slaves to debt. Please save my future husband from this trap. I pray he is so content in life, that he never feels the need to keep up with what others have. I pray he is secure in his relationship with You that he is not compelled to buy out of a longing to be satisfied. If he has any habits that do not help him be a good steward of finances, please transform this part of him. Transform his mind and help him to understand the truth about money.

In Jesus' name AMEN!

Making Wise Decisions

Proverbs 12:15

Dear Lord,

I pray my future husband is a man who fears You. I pray Your Holy presence is evident in his life. Please continue to mature his character, grow his heart, feed him truth and guard his mind. I pray he prays and asks You for wisdom. I pray You would send righteous men to influence him in Your ways and advise him to pursue righteousness in all his decision making. I pray my future husband is a humble man who listens to wise advice. If there is any foolishness in his heart, I pray You would remove it. Till the soil of his heart so that the fruits of Your Spirit may flourish. I pray he would never fight to be right, but rather, I pray he would fight for truth, Your truth. May Your Holy Spirit show him when he is seeking after validation for himself so that he will change. I also pray that he never fights to be right in our marriage. I pray he would be humble and navigate our future conversations with compassion and in pursuit of understanding. Please remove any pride from his heart that would hinder him from being a compassionate and humble husband. I pray that we both would seek to make wise choices in our marriage. With every decision we have to make, help us to make them together with peace guarding our hearts and Your wisdom leading us.

In Jesus' name AMEN!

Challenge

— #3 —

WRITE
God a letter

Share with Him your whole heart.

Include your hopes and fears for marriage, and
what you are currently feeling or experiencing.

His Health

1 Corinthians 6:19-20

Dear God,

I pray for my future husband's health. Thank You for his life. Thank You for his heart. I pray he would trust You with his body. I pray if he ever gets sick, that You would comfort him and heal him quickly. If he suffers from any chronic disease or pain, please reach down and touch him! Heal him completely and may the miracle of healing be an incredible testimony of Your power and love. I pray he would choose to abstain from things in this world that would hurt his body or cause addiction. If he is doing something to his body that he shouldn't be, I pray Your Holy Spirit would speak to him about the matter and provide ample education and conviction that would convince him to stop. Remind him that he can't fight the desires of the flesh without You. Help him to rely on You for recovery, restoration and victory. I pray my future husband is a modest man and that the way he dresses honors You. I pray he submits his body to You as an offering. I pray he uses the talents you have given to him and the skills he has acquired to bless You and worship You. Remind him that his body is a gift from You and that he should treat it with utmost respect. I pray my future husband would be an advocate for healthy living. I pray he is passionate about eating healthy and exercise so that vitality is abundant in him. May his lifestyle reflect his desire to honor You with his body.

In Jesus' name AMEN!

Integrity

Proverbs 10:9

Dear Lord,

I pray my future husband lives a life full of integrity. May he walk in righteousness all the days of his life. I pray he has strong morals that are founded in Your Holy Word. I pray he is an honest man and that everything he does is done with honesty. May his words and his actions be genuine and sincere. Holy Spirit, refine him so that he is a man of virtue. I pray he upholds Biblical standards of truth. I pray he has a conviction to live a life that is noble and pure. I pray my future husband would walk securely, all the days of his life, because he has integrity in his heart always motivating him to do what is right. I pray he respects the elderly and those in authority. I pray he treats women well with compassion and understanding. I pray he has a heart of tenderness toward children. I pray he is a leader among men and that he stands out because he is a defender of truth and a bright light shining in such a dark world. If there is a part of his character that does not have integrity, I pray You would remove it from him. Transform him into a man of courage who is willing to be set apart from this world. I pray my future husband clings to the truth, now, and into our marriage. I pray he leads me in this area and teaches me by the example of the godly life he lives out each and every day.

In Jesus' name AMEN!

Resisting Temptation

1 Corinthians 10:13

Dear God,

Thank You for always providing a way out of temptation. Thank You for Your faithfulness. I pray my future husband strives to be faithful in all he does. I pray that when he is tempted, he is able to resist it and seek after You. I pray he is so sensitive to the Holy Spirit that he would see the escape You provide from temptation. I pray for this area of his life, especially during the times that he is alone and feels weak. Remind him that You are near and that You will give him the strength to resist the temptation to sin. Remind him that he can flee whatever situation he is in. I pray that in a moment of weakness, instead of being enticed to sin, he would call a friend or a mentor who would remove him from where he is at and that he break the cycle of giving into his flesh. Surround him with good people and strong friends who also have a desire to live righteously. I pray You would help my future husband endure the circumstances he is confronted by. I pray for wisdom to flood his heart and mind in times that he needs to make decisions. I pray against the enemy and his schemes to tempt my future husband to sin. May Your perfect will be done in his life.

In Jesus' name AMEN!

Invest

Relati

In
onships

Don't let loneliness overwhelm you, invest in the relationships you have with family and friends. Most of all be confident and satisfied in in your relationship with God in Christ Jesus.

Love Like Christ

John 15:12-13

Dear Heavenly Father,

Thank You for Your beautiful example of love. Thank You for loving me and thank You for loving my future husband. I am in awe of the power of love and how it can transform life. I pray my future husband has an incredibly intimate relationship with You. I pray he knows what real love is because he knows You. Holy Spirit, please fill his heart with Your presence and help him to love like Christ. I pray he can love and lay down his life for his friends. I pray he is motivated by Your love to love all people. Open his eyes and reveal to him every day how he can bless others. I pray he is willing to sacrifice his desires for the sake of others. May You inspire him to always go the extra mile to bless those around him. I pray he also has a great love for me. I pray our love would grow deeply intimate and that what we experience together helps us understand the way You love us too. I pray my future husband loves unconditionally. I pray he is affectionate and understanding. I pray he is creative in the way that he tells me and shows me that he loves me. I pray that he is blessed by all the ways You allow him to love the people You have placed in his life. I pray love rejuvenates his soul and reminds him just how much You love him. I pray he never doubts Your great love for him.

In Jesus' name AMEN!

Being A Good Steward

1 Corinthians 4:1

Dear Lord,

Thank You for all of Your good and precious gifts. Thank You for Your provision. I pray for my future husband today. I pray he would acknowledge and appreciate all of the gifts You provide for him. I pray he would be a good steward of Your provision. May he make wise decisions with all that You give to him. May he be satisfied whether You bless him with more than enough or just barely enough. I pray he would be grateful for all of it. I pray there are people in his life right now that will help guide him in ways that honor You. May there be people in his life who are intentional about teaching him how to use all that You provide. I pray he would be a good servant. I pray his heart is softened toward those in need. I pray my future husband is a generous man. I pray he is willing to give good gifts to others. I pray he manages his life so well, that he has time, energy and resources to help those in his community. I pray for our future marriage. May Your Holy Spirit help my husband lead us as we make decisions together. I pray we will always encourage each other to use our marriage to bless others, to use our gifts to bless others and to use our resources to fulfill the needs of others. May You remind us daily that what we have in this life has been granted by You.

In Jesus' name AMEN!

Challenge
— #4 —

WRITE
another letter

This time a response to your letter to God,
from God's perspective.

What do you think He would say
to encourage you?

Good Company

Proverbs 13:20

Dear God,

Thank You for the gift of friendship. I pray my future husband keeps good company around. I pray he has friends that are wise, people who will direct him and encourage him to make good choices. I pray his friends and him have relationship boundaries and that they respect each other's boundaries. I pray my future husband would be an encouragement to his friends and that he would be an ambassador of Your Word to them. I also pray they would speak truth into his life. I pray his friendships benefit his character and motivate him to be a good man. May he continue to grow up and become wiser because of the wise influences in his life. I pray his friends are examples of good citizenship and respect the law. I pray his friends know You and love You, and if they don't know You, may they come to know You through the love my future husband has for You. I pray my future husband has strong friendships that he can count on. I pray they are lifelong friends who will always challenge each other to be better men. I pray my future husband feels the love of his friends because they tell him and show him that they love him. I also pray he is the best friend anyone could ever have. I pray we will be the best of friends. May Your will be done in his life and in the friendships he has.

In Jesus' name AMEN!

Saying No To Pornography

Psalm 119:37

Dear Lord,

This world is growing darker. It is becoming more and more acceptable to advertise and entertain using pornography. The accessibility of pornography and the ability to hide it is becoming easier than ever. I pray that in this day and age when pornography is paraded around as something good, my future husband would resist the temptation of pornography. I pray You would guard his eyes against seeing it. I pray You would convict his heart on media that use it as entertainment. I pray You would reveal the devastating truth of all that pornography destroys. I pray my future husband would be an advocate for purity. I pray he would protect our future marriage by abstaining from looking at pornography. I also pray he would protect his mind and heart by vigorously opposing it. Remind him to lean on You for strength when he feels weak in this area of his life. May his heart never justify that kind of sin. I pray Your truth is made clear to him and that his perspective on this topic is shaped by Your truth. I pray he would respect women and honor them, always. I pray he would say no to pornography and turn his eyes from looking at anything that does not glorify You. I pray my future husband would seek after purity and fight for it at all cost. May he be a light in the lives of the men around him to also seek purity. I pray for victory in this area of his life, for the rest of his life.

In Jesus' name AMEN!

Dying To Self

Luke 9:23

Dear Heavenly Father,

To serve You and to follow You is a great honor. Your love is real and Your grace is amazing. Thank You for being an example of true love. Thank You for sacrificing Yourself so that we may be reconciled to You. Thank You for the gift of true intimacy. I pray for the heart of my future husband. I pray that he desires to follow You. I pray he passionately pursues You every day for the rest of his life. May Your Holy Spirit teach him how to love like You love. Teach him how to deny his flesh and follow in Your footsteps. May he be willing to serve You all the days of his life. I pray he serves You joyfully. I pray that You prepare his heart for our future marriage. Mold him and shape him into the husband You desire him to be. May You help him see that marriage requires he deny himself and die to himself to embrace oneness in our marriage. I pray You would strip selfishness and pride from his heart. I pray he would learn how to live as one with me. Help me to die to myself to be one with him. I pray we would surrender our wills to fulfill Your will for our marriage. No matter what challenges or obstacles we face, I pray we make it through them together. I pray no conflict would be so great that it would tear us apart. Help both of us to persevere with hopefulness and love leading our hearts.

In Jesus' name AMEN!

Plan
for

ning

love

So many people get caught up in the details of their wedding day that they forget to focus on their future marriage. Planning for your wedding should be fun, but also invest in your future marriage by planning creative ways to love your future husband!

Working Hard

Colossians 3:23-24

Dear Lord,

I pray my future husband is a hard worker. I pray he is willing to labor over any job opportunity You provide for him. I am sure there will also be requests made for his help on jobs outside of work and after hours. I pray he is wise about whether or not to agree to help others, but that his heart is always willing. I pray for balance in his life in the area of work. I pray he feels content and satisfied in his job. I also pray You help him navigate any transitions that come up because of work. Any jobs or career my future husband pursues, I pray he works hard with all of his heart as if he is working for You. I pray that in his work he glorifies You. I pray he gives You the glory for the achievements he makes, knowing it was You who helped him. I pray he also is never afraid to be a light in his workplace. I pray he encourages his co-workers and points them toward You. I pray he never finds himself in a demanding job that requires him to deny You or requires him to do something that is contrary to what You want him to do. I pray he never uses sin, such as lying or manipulation, to get ahead in his career. May honesty always be his policy. I pray You would bless my future husband in any job that he does. Bless him with good pay that affirms his job well done, bless him with an ever expanding wealth of knowledge and increase blessing over him wherever he goes that his employer also reaps a harvest that can be attributed back to You with rejoicing.

In Jesus' name AMEN!

Striving For Purity

Hebrews 13:4

31 Prayers For My Future Husband

Dear Heavenly Father,

You say in Your Word that marriage should be honored by all and the marriage bed kept pure. I pray my future husband exercises obedience in this area of his life. May he pursue purity in every aspect of his life. I pray he is sexually pure, that his language is pure and his thoughts and intentions are pure. If he struggles with purity in any way, please transform him in a radical way. Send other men into his life who will encourage him to be pure. I pray with any relationship or friendship he has, that he would place boundaries to protect his purity. I pray he has a correct perspective of marriage and that he sees marriage as a gift from You. May he encourage other married couples with words of affirmation every chance he gets. I pray he would see his commitment to marriage as serious. I pray he has a conviction in his heart to strive for purity even after we say "I do!" I pray the choices he makes now, sets up our marriage relationship in a way that is healthy and holy. May his desire for holiness far outweigh any desire of his flesh. If he wrestles with anything unclean, impure, addictive or unhealthy, please break the chains of bondage in his life. Clean out the garbage and replace it with Your Holy presence. I pray my future husband does everything in his power and while relying on You for strength to pursue purity in this crooked and perverse generation. May his life be refreshing to others around him and may he testify how good life is because of You. I pray his strength to resist sin is appealing to others, and when they inquire and ask why he is so different he points them to You!

In Jesus' name AMEN!

A Heart Of Compassion

Colossians 3:12-14

Dear Lord,

Thank You for today. I praise You God, because You are good and Your love is everlasting. Thank You for Your grace. I pray my future husband would experience Your amazing grace. I pray Your grace would transform his life in a miraculous way. I pray he would devour Your Word in a way that it saturates every part of his soul. May he learn about Your compassionate heart and may he long to have such a heart. I pray he discovers the character You have and that he desires to have the same. Inspire him to live according to Your ways. I pray he is compassionate, caring, kind and patient. I pray he forgives easily knowing that You have forgiven him. I pray he is a man who loves well. May he have a compassionate heart toward those who need help and who are hurting. May his compassion motivate him to action. Holy Spirit, may You infuse his mind with creative ways to be a blessing to others and to use the gifts and resources You have given him to bless others. I pray You would give him an extra portion of compassion for me when we get married. I pray his heart would be sensitive toward me. I pray that any difficult trial we experience as husband and wife, we can persevere through because of compassion. I pray the suffering we may endure would motivate our hearts to help each other and to encourage each other along the way.

In Jesus' name AMEN!

Challenge

— #5 —

UNVEIL YOUR
heart to God

Let Him get to know you, especially the parts
that you are good at hiding.

If there is sin in your life, take a moment
to repent and be reconciled to God.

Victory In Christ

1 Corinthians 15:57

Dear Lord,

This world is growing darker, evil is rampant and the enemy is on the prowl. This world is a battlefield. I pray my future husband would follow Your lead. I pray he would taste the goodness of victory in You. Even though evil tempts him to turn his heart against You and Your Church, may he know the truth and may he stand strong in the day of adversity. Thank You Lord, for victory in Christ. Thank You for always helping. I pray my future husband would rely on You for help. I pray he knows what victory in Christ is. Liberate him from the bondage of sin. Set him free from the grip of the enemy. Protect him from any advances the enemy takes against him. I pray my future husband would experience achievement and growth. I pray he would overcome evil and resist temptation. I pray he would recognize all of the moments You give him more strength, more wisdom, more courage, more patience and more knowledge to overcome the hardest things in his life. May he glorify You and praise You. Please continue to equip him for this battle. I pray my future husband is familiar with Your armor and that he uses it every day to fight the good fight of faith. When we get married, I pray he continues to experience victory in Christ. I pray he passionately fights for our marriage. Help him and use him to subdue the enemy.

In Jesus' name AMEN!

Becoming A Leader

Hebrews 13:7

Dear Heavenly Father,

I pray that my future husband has leaders around him who know Your Word well and live it out in obedience every day. I pray they walk with him closely, advising him in Your ways. I pray their way of life is an awesome example to him on how to be a mature man, a wise man, a man of love, a man of honor and a man of righteousness. I pray my future husband would imitate their ways. I pray he would observe and learn from the godly examples he has in his life. Surround him with many good examples. I pray he would become a leader. I pray he would lead other young men in Your Word and Your ways. I pray my future husband would walk in obedience. I pray he would be keen on the direction You provide for him. May Your Holy Spirit guide his heart in Your will and purpose for his life. I pray he would have a humble perspective as a leader and that he leads with a servant's heart. Anoint my future husband with wisdom and knowledge. Delight in his steps. Develop his character and develop his ability to discern. I pray my future husband is an observant man, slow to speak and slow to become angry. Give him a peaceful heart and a mind that is focused on pleasing You. May You equip him to lead me as a strong and loving husband. Increase his confidence and may he lead well.

In Jesus' name AMEN!

Relinquishing Worries

Philippians 4:6-7

Dear God,

Thank You for today. I lift up my future husband to You right now. I pray that if there is anything burdening his heart he would submit it to You. I pray that if he is overwhelmed or worried he would find peace in You. Bless his heart, Lord. I pray my future husband is quick to come to You in prayer. I pray he is able to relinquish his worries. Help him not to be anxious about anything, but in everything may he pray and petition, with thanksgiving, present his requests to You. I pray that if he is wrestling with sin, is pressured to make a decision or just has great concern for the things that are happening in other people's lives, I pray he is able to surrender everything to You. I pray You would remove any anxious thoughts and replace them with Your amazing peace. Fill his mind and his heart with Your peace. Give him understanding about the things he is struggling with. Help him to find freedom, victory, solutions and other encouragement. Guard his heart, Lord. Build up his faith. Show him the power of prayer. Reveal to him how much You care about all the things he thinks about, all the encounters and experiences he has, all of the details of his life. Tell him over and over again how much You desire to hear from him through prayer. I pray my future husband is a humble man who prays to You every day of his life. Help him not to worry. Help him not to fear. Teach him to pray and teach him to be thankful for everything.

In Jesus' name AMEN!

You

Bea

Are

utiful

You are beautiful inside and out! God made you with intentional thought and extraordinary purpose. Don't seek approval and validation from the world, rather seek God and find security in Him alone.

Living With Understanding

Proverbs 4:7

Dear Heavenly Father,

Thank You for my future husband. I pray that if it is in Your will, I marry him at Your appointed time for us. I pray a blessing over my future husband. I pray he is filled with Your Holy Spirit. I pray he is anointed by Your Holy Spirit. May You continue to mature his faith and his character. I pray he allows You to go to the deep places in his heart and heal him from any past wounds he may have. Make him whole. I pray he would allow all of his experiences to shape who he is and I pray what he learns along the way gives him an awesome perspective of life. I pray he is a man of compassion and understanding. I pray he is a man full of Your wisdom. I pray that he prays for wisdom and believes that You will increase what he knows. I pray he is a man who is always humble and willing to learn from everyone he meets. I pray he does everything he can to gain understanding. I pray he is eager to absorb information. I pray he has a desire to be educated. I pray he is a man that pursues knowledge whether in his relationship with You, his job, his friendships, his hobbies or with me. I pray that in our future marriage, he would live with me with understanding and that he would teach me the things he knows. May we grow closer together because of his desire to live with understanding.

In Jesus' name AMEN!

Fruit Of The Spirit

Galatians 5:22-23

Dear Lord,

Thank You for the Holy Spirit. The Holy Spirit is an incredible gift You have given to the world. I pray my future husband embraces the gift of the Holy Spirit. I pray he allows the Holy Spirit to lead him and transform him. I pray my future husband's character is a reflection of Your Holy character. May the fruits of the Spirit be evident in his life. I pray my future husband is full of love, great love, deep love. Like a well that never dries up! I pray he has contagious joy. I pray that others who are around him would feel his joy radiating from his heart. I pray peace covers him like a warm blanket, always bringing comfort to him and those around him. I pray he is a patient man, slow to become frustrated no matter what the circumstance is. I pray he is genuinely kind to everyone. I pray kindness motivates his every action and every word. I pray that goodness is abundant in his life as he pursues righteousness. I pray he has a conviction to be a man of faithfulness. I pray gentleness is tangible in the way that he experiences the sense of touch and that aggression is far from his heart. I pray my future husband has self-control in every area of his life. I pray that he has beneficial habits that add to the health and wellness of his body, mind and soul. I pray that anyone around him gets to taste the goodness of You because the fruits of the Spirit are always abundant in his life.

In Jesus' name AMEN!

Maturing Him

1 Corinthians 14:20

Dear Heavenly Father,

You are powerful! You are creative! You are intentional! You mold people's hearts like a potter molds clay. I pray my future husband has such a personal and intimate relationship with You that he lets You mold him into the man You created him to be. You have such a great purpose for his life. Reveal to him what that purpose is and reveal to him why You gave him the talents and skills he has. I pray he would be a man of maturity. I pray he would think clearly, act respectfully and love deeply. I pray he would put childish ways behind him and embrace his responsibilities as an adult. I pray he is sophisticated, intelligent and capable. I pray he is still playful and desires to have fun, but also knows when to be serious. Bring balance to his life and a clear understanding of manhood. Help him to embrace his role as a man and all that You have called him to. I pray that when we get married, he would embrace his role as a husband and be willing to lead me. Holy Spirit, please anoint my future husband, maturing him and shaping him into a man who fears You. I pray he operates in selflessness and humility, yet has the confidence to stand on his convictions that are based on Your truth. Mature his character, his perspective, his attitude, everything. Transform his heart and prepare him for all that You have for him.

In Jesus' name AMEN!

Challenge

— # 6 —

SPEND TIME
in prayer

Spend 31 minutes praying only for your
future husband and your future marriage.

Humility

Philippians 2:3-11

Dear Lord,

I pray my future husband is a humble man. I pray he would not be conceited or seek self-gain. If there is selfishness in his heart, please remove it! Give him eyes to see others, to help others, serve others, love others and put other's needs above his own. I pray that in every circumstance or situation he faces he would exercise humility in his responses. I pray he would never grow weary of doing good. I pray my future husband is a man who seeks to be like Christ in every way. Reveal to him how Christ walked in humility. Reveal to him the importance of humility. I pray my future husband honors You and admires who You are, always chasing after Your heart. Lord, please help him to be a husband who walks in humility. I pray he reacts and responds to me with a humble heart. I pray he is willing to work through things with me, motivated to understand me and what I am going through. I also pray that I would be humble and motivated to understand him. May pride never get in the way of him doing what is right. I pray he is never afraid to ask for help, show his weakness or express his emotions. I pray pride has no place in his heart. I pray he is meek and gentle, but also brave and assertive. I pray he is a man who knows his significance and value. I pray he knows how much he is loved.

In Jesus' name AMEN!

Preparing His Heart

Ephesians 5:22-28

Dear Heavenly Father,

Thank You for my future husband. I pray You would give me patience as I await the day we are united as one. Until that joyous moment comes, please prepare my future husband's heart for our marriage. I pray You would shape him into the husband You created him to be. I pray he would have a profound understanding of what it means to be a husband and how You desire him to fulfill that role. May he be eager to love me like You love. May he lead me as You have called him to. Make him strong and make him wise. I pray he would know You well and know Your Word well. I pray he would live his life according to Your ways and that his life is a strong testimony of who You are. I pray he is honored and respected by others. I pray he would have a heart to serve others. Most of all, I pray his heart is surrendered to You in every way. I pray that he trusts You confidently. I pray he would be a man of integrity. May he be slow to become angry. I pray the fruits of the Spirit are evident in his life. Prepare his heart for oneness. We both have been living for ourselves, which is something that I know will change when we marry. Help us both to be willing to live together in harmony, looking out for each other and living in an understanding way. I pray his heart would be excited about marriage and the gift of oneness we will share.

In Jesus' name AMEN!

Intimacy With God

John 14:21

Dear God,

Thank You for the gift of intimacy. I pray my future husband takes advantage of every day he is given to spend time with You. I pray he is passionate about serving You. May Your Holy Spirit mature him and fill him with wisdom as he pursues an intimate relationship with You. I pray he is determined to keep Your commandments. I pray he is a man of obedience. May his heart long to draw ever closer to You! I pray that I would also continue to experience deep intimacy in my relationship with You. I pray we have an understanding that You are the most important thing in this life, even above our marriage. I pray we never sacrifice our time with You. I pray that we both allow You into the deepest, darkest parts of our hearts. I pray for courage to be transparent with You and let You really get to know us. I pray against feelings of shame and guilt from sin or embarrassment that would hinder us from coming to You or hinder You from knowing us well. If my future husband needs healing for anything in his past, I pray that the intimacy You and him experience would lead to that healing soon. I also pray that if I have any raw wounds from my past and need healing, I would experience that soon. Prepare our hearts for one another by mending any brokenness or pain we have endured from our past. I pray our daily commitment to reading Your Word and praying would satisfy us and help us experience intimacy with You like we never have before.

In Jesus' name AMEN!

Love Y

ourself

Love your future husband today by loving yourself. Take care of yourself, seek an intimate relationship with God, protect your purity and be confident in the purposes God has for you.

Our Future Wedding

Revelation 19:6-9

Dear Lord,

I pray for our future wedding. I pray our families would support us throughout the planning process and celebration. May Your Holy Spirit calm any storms that try and tear down Your will for our future relationship. I pray for peace and I pray the enemy is removed far from us. Stop any attacks he plots against us. Help my future husband and me to purpose our wedding celebration around You, glorifying You in every way. I pray that all those who attend our wedding would feel You near. I pray our wedding goes smooth with no accidents, conflicts or hiccups. Holy Spirit, be at the center of it all! Anoint our union as husband and wife. Thank You for the future wedding You have prepared for Christ and Your Church. Your love story is so beautiful. I pray my future husband and I will be present that day to celebrate and rejoice with You. I also pray that anyone who witnesses our wedding and marriage would come to know You more and ultimately be present at Your future wedding. I pray our hearts are always turned toward You. I pray my future husband leads me to understand You more. Prepare his heart as the spiritual leader of our family and prepare my heart to follow his lead and support him. May You be glorified through our relationship and may others draw closer to You because of what they see in us.

In Jesus' name AMEN!

Our Future Marriage

Ecclesiastes 4:9-12

Dear God,

Thank You for the incredible gift of marriage. Thank You for designing marriage with such detail and thoughtfulness. Thank You for giving me a desire to marry and for teaching me how marriage is a reflection of Your beautiful love story. I pray that hope in my heart for marriage never ceases. Thank You for my future husband. I pray a blessing over our future marriage. I pray our relationship draws us closer to You. I pray that we would embrace the intimacy You created us to have. May Your Holy Spirit guide us through marriage, teaching us how to live out our roles as husband and wife. Increase our desire for each other and inspire us with creative ways to show each other love every single day. May our marriage help us to grow together as a team, where we encourage each other through life's ups and downs. I pray that we die to ourselves and live to defend our marriage. I pray we are faithful to You and each other with every ounce of our beings. May we never feel lonely, left out or neglected by each other. I pray we would serve You together and that we would pursue Your will for our lives. I pray we remain passionate about our relationship and that both of us would be brave enough to initiate and pursue intimacy. I pray against the enemy and his evil attacks against our relationship. Fortify us, Lord. Make us strong. Keep our hearts focused and founded on You.

In Jesus' name AMEN!

Our Future Oneness

Genesis 2:22-24

Dear Lord,

Thank You for my future marriage. I pray my future husband and I would grow to understand what it means to be one with each other. I pray he would be able to leave his family and be united to me. I pray I am able to leave my family and cleave to him. I pray You would unite us as one, bind our hearts together in holiness and harmony, knit our hearts together as husband and wife. May Your Holy Spirit guide us into deep conversations that help us discover the purpose of oneness in marriage. I pray we would be transparent with each other as we share the deepest parts of our hearts with each other. Inspire us to initiate conversations that matter. Give us courage and strength to walk in humility every day. May Your Holy Spirit motivate us to keep our relationship as a significant priority in our lives. I pray we would experience indescribable joy and abundant unconditional love in our marriage. I pray we would satisfy each other in every way. I pray we would complement each other. I pray we reflect Your amazing grace and Your extraordinary love. Remind us every day that we are one with each other and one with You! I pray we would always be willing to operate as one, living with understanding, passionately pursuing peace every day we spend together. Lord, may Your will be done in us and through us as we pursue You and strive to fulfill Your will in our marriage.

In Jesus' name AMEN!

Challenge

— #7 —

WRITE
him a letter

Write a letter to your future husband.

Hold on to this until your wedding day,
then give it to him as a special gift.

31 Prayers For My Future Husband

Vows

My husband and I decided not to write our own vows when we got married. We went the traditional route and repeated the words our Pastor lead. Looking back at our wedding and our relationship, there are some things we would have said if we did write our own vows. As we celebrate our 10th wedding anniversary January 6th, 2017, we decided to write out the words that we felt when we made our commitment to marriage, along with some words we have grown to understand deeper as we have experienced the richness of marriage over the last 10 years. We wanted to share these with you to inspire your heart to deeply consider the significance of your vows; whether you decide to make your commitment to marriage by using traditional vows, writing your own vows or using these that we are sharing with you! Vows are a vital part of the wedding process and the words you say on the altar are the foundation of your marriage covenant.

Vows To Him

You are my best friend, forever.

I thank God for bringing you into my life.

You have shown me true love, and you have influenced my life for the better.

Thank you for choosing me to be yours alone.

Thank you for loving me like Christ.

Thank you for believing in my talents, and thank you for always pointing me toward God.

You are my biggest encourager, you are my greatest source of comfort besides God, and you are my favorite person in this world.

You are my answer to prayer.

I don't know what our future holds, but I do know God has big plans for us.

I know because we are both dreamers for His Kingdom and we desire to serve Him with everything we have.

I can't guarantee that we will never face hardship or unwanted trials, in fact, I am more positive that we will face challenges in this life, but as your wife, I promise to persevere together with you.

I promise to understand what it means to be one with you.
I promise to follow you and let you lead me and lead our family.

I promise to do my part to leave a legacy of love.

I promise to always point your heart toward God.

I promise to support your faith and encourage your love for the Lord.

I also promise to surrender my heart to God and pursue my own relationship with Him.

I promise to rely on Him to fulfill me and I commit to being obedient to His Word.

I promise to let Him change my heart so that I can be the wife He wants me to be for you.

I commit to learning and always investing into our marriage.

I promise to be respectful in my responses, and I promise to seek reconciliation with you at any sign of discord or tension.

I promise to cheer you on in life, to comfort you, to exhort you in your God-given desires. I promise to be faithful.

I promise to be loyal.
I promise to fight for our marriage.

I may never be perfect, but I promise to always strive for perfection and victory won through Christ alone.

I promise to hold your hand for as long as you want and grow old by your side, unless Jesus comes back before then.

I promise to love you through sickness, through doubt, through drought, and through financial depression.

I promise to stick closer than glue.

I commit my heart to finding security in God and not in the things of this world.

I commit to loving you despite our circumstances and whether or not our marriage is everything we ever hope for.

I promise to have fun with you and to laugh with you.

I promise to pray with you and pray for you.

I vow to intentionally pursue intimacy with you, and I commit my whole heart to loving you extravagantly.

I promise to give you my heart, to let you see the real me.

I promise to always be transparent with you, and I promise to share the deepest parts of me with you.

I promise to let you get to know me and I promise to spend time getting to know you, for the rest of our lives.

I promise to give you permission to speak truth into my life, to tell me when you see sin in my life, and I promise to purpose my heart to listen to you.

I promise to keep Christ at the center of our relationship, the foundation and cornerstone of our covenant.

A cord of three strands is not quickly broken.

You, me and Christ are intimately intertwined.

I promise, that even in our brokenness, I will hold on to what we have and never let it go.

I promise to make our marriage the most important priority in our life. I promise to pursue oneness with you.

I promise to pursue an extraordinary life with you.

I promise to do my part in our love story and love you well.

I promise to be your best friend, forever.

I love you and I always will, I promise.

Vows To Her

I may never be able to give you the life you deserve.

I may never be able to give you the things your heart desires.

I may never be able to build you a dream home.

I may never have a bank account filled with money.

I know that there will be hard times and painful times.

I know there will be moments of doubt and fear.

There are many things that I will never be able to do for you, but the things that I can do I promise to do with all my heart.

I promise to love you even when you are unloveable and when I feel like I can't love anymore.

I promise to ask God to help me love you.

I promise to take care of you and our family to the best of my ability.

I promise to make you a priority over everything else in my life.

I promise to tell you anything and to let you tell me anything.

I will never stop pursuing my walk with God and my faith in His Son, Jesus Christ.

I will do everything I can to make Jesus the center of our marriage and home.

I promise to ask God daily to make our marriage into a powerful tool for His Kingdom. I will always have eyes for you and you alone.

I will always speak well of you to others, and I promise to encourage you. I promise to keep my heart pure for you.

I pray the Holy Spirit would keep me always growing closer to God and you.

I will protect our oneness at all cost.

I promise to keep my covenant with you always.

You are my gift and a promise fulfilled, and I will always be thankful and excited to have and to hold you.

I promise to steward your heart well in the strength God gives me every day.

Thank you for waiting for me.

Thank you for saying yes to God, and thank you for saying yes to me.

I love you.

Marriage After God

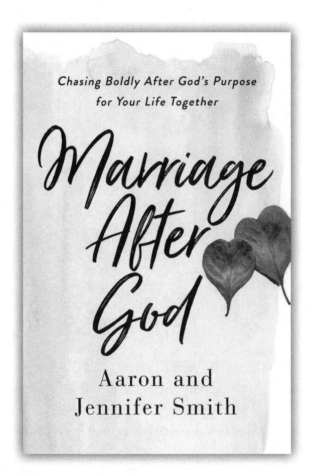

Getting married soon? Start your marriage off with a strong foundation and grab a copy of Marriage After God today!

MarriageAfterGod.com

Thirty-One Prayers For Your Spouse

Don't stop praying for your spouse after you get married make prayer a daily habit and a life long pursuit.

Husband & Wife After God 30-Day Devotionals

These two complementary marriage devotionals walk through important biblical marriage principles, while also addressing different areas of life that a husband and wife might struggle with. We wrote these devotionals to help husbands and wives grow closer to God and closer to each other.

Visit Our Online Book Store Today.
Shop.MarriageAfterGod.com

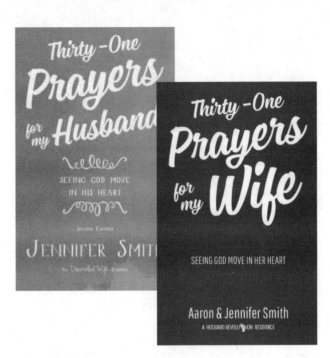

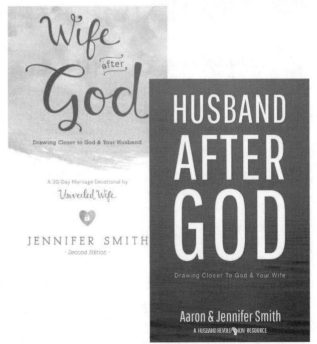

If this prayer book has impacted your faith please let me know by posting a testimony here:

31prayersformyfuturehusband.com

For more marriage resources please visit:

shop.MarriageAfterGod.com

Signup for daily prayers by email:

dailymarriageprayer.com

Get connected:

Facebook.com/unveiledwife

Pinterest.com/unveiledwife

Youtube.com/unveiledwife

Instagram.com/unveiledwife

Twitter.com/unveiledwife